Real-Life Fiction

Edwin Torres

PAGE PUBLISHING, INC.
Conneaut Lake, PA

First originally published by Page Publishing 2020

ISBN 978-1-64628-723-9 (pbk)
ISBN 978-1-64628-724-6 (digital)

Printed in the United States of America

I would like to thank Holly Ickes, Sal Furlock, and everyone on the page publishing staff for making this book possible. I would also like to thank the readers who took time out to read this book.

Sincerely Yours Truly: Edwin Torres

Contents

Afterlife

Do I have a spot reserved in heaven
If I don't it means I do not deserve to get in.
Tell the gods I'm coming
After all their jobs are done with.
Should I ask a price
To be visible in the afterlife
Or come back tonight
Even if everything is black and white.
What I would give to be in the earth
Relive my life even if the reasons will hurt
Bring me back in the form of an animal free like a bird
I'll sleep in the dirt
Get my nutrition from plants
Because I'm eating the herbs.
Let it be known to some of my makers
That I want to be at one with the nature.
The world would be reborn at my feet
Rejoin the world in the form of a tree
Give life provide food and oxygen
For those who got to win
No longer looking for green
Because I've got lots of it
Make the world
The way it would not have been.
The rain makes my roots flourish
So I can help humanity nourish.
I'll be the protector
Of all of God's creatures
Even the ones with odd features.
Only hunt to survive
Protect all living things
In front of my eyes
In the afterlife

I want to have four legs and a tail
And watch the world move ahead and prevail
The jungle is my home
The tail keeps me balanced
So to be stumbling I won't.
I want to have every animal's race endured up
To communicate with them like Ace Ventura.
I love all living things
Even love hearing children sing
In the next life
I hope the gods give me wings.
If I was the king of the animal kingdom
I'll tell my fellow creatures
That we're facing extinction.
The human race is to fear
Because they're making us disappear.
All wildlife is enjoying the planet
But we're the ones destroying the planet.
So I'll see you in the afterlife.

Allegory

Pay attention to this allegory
They only told half the story
I'm going past the glory
Writing this like it's mandatory.
What they didn't mention to you
Is that we're in a temple of doom
It's why every move is detrimental to move.
When I'm playing the game
I'm not saying no names
Just stay in the lane
Every day is insane,
And every thought is cynical
It's about to get critical
I've got to pass the physical
About to get political.
And I know it's complicated
Work like you're obligated
Until your rights are confiscated
Now you're feeling dominated
They want to envy on this hate it
Every single promise made it.
But never fulfilled
Just combats and wrongful kills.
This is what we're hating
We keep debating
Not creating or relating
Send the poor to prison
In these states united
It's a lot more division
If you hate to fight it
Then do it with a vision
Tell me what you've sighted
Let's start the mission.

Writing my chronicles
Overcome any obstacles
In a world cold like Popsicles
People dying in hospitals
Everyone feeling hostile
Even the ones singing gospels
With a crew of apostles.
Tell them the truth
And blow off the roof
The word will go off my tooth
This is the proof
No future for the youth.
I'm not writing a melody
Because then I'll be fighting a felony.
If I drop an album
Then I'll get shot like Malcolm
That is not my outcome.
Collecting dust for years
No more trust is here
Put what they must in ears
Money lust and fear
The end for us is near.
Days are short and nights are long
Can't tell the difference from right and wrong
Or right from left
Just fight to death
Take the lightest breath
Can't see or hear they lost sight they're deaf.

Have a drink in my name
While I sink in my pain
They all think I'm insane
Even the shrinks know my name
Always in ink it remains
Doing it fast in a blink it just came
With no links to the chain.

Back in the Day

I remember when we bought two bazookas with a dime
Basketball was at its prime
Rappers were real with the rhymes
Yes I know those were the times.
We would walk to Isaac
On our way stop and buy shit.
In a fun crew at the lunchroom
Believing things that were untrue.
But the rumors
Were spread sooner.
On our way to class
Man how those days have passed
Wish they would replay and last
So back then they would pay your ass.
Every Friday play ball at Jeff
Until nighttime
Or they all have left.
To us it was about pride
The way we held it down outside
And I enjoyed south side.
Yes took it indoors
When it was cold out
No one would hold out
Real people wouldn't have sold out.
And it's time to say
It wasn't designed this way
I have better things in my lines to say.

High school was worthless
The principle ringleader of the circus
Like any business it's just a service
They haven't heard this.
High school was a damaged past.
Put a Spanish kid in a Spanish class.
I know easy A
But not what I need today
To help me lead the way
Real education what I read and say.
That was back in the day.

Being Alive

The point of being alive
Is to always strive to survive
And thrive and arrive.
In a new life wish I could restart it all
So I can do something remarkable
Establish my own mark and all
It's not about money cars and all.
This life isn't about being rich
It's about finding your niche
It hasn't made anything switch
We're seeing life with a glitch
Until we're under a ditch.
Work with what you've got
And know you're deserving of a lot
You are worthy of the top
Keep going and don't stop
Unless you've dropped.
This life just live it
When you want to surrender
Don't give in
You're the contender.
Just keep going
Like the wind blowing
In a destination not knowing.
Where you might end up
The heavens are calling
Tonight I'm getting sent up
When the bad times arise
Look at them in your eyes
And don't act surprised.
Take it in the brain who's to blame
For all the pain.
I feel from the heart

It's been real from the start
The pain won't heal or depart.
Inside have an empty hole
Love with a heavy soul
But when it's getting cold.
And have no one to keep you warm
You want to be reborn
Because inside you're being torn.
It feels like a lot to know
Very fast not to slow
From here you got to grow.
And focus on being alive.

Critical Judgement

If we smoke weed
We get criticized
It's what we don't need
They get minimized.
So if you drink a Bud Light
I let the Bud Light
Spark in the dark
Now the session starts
Don't hit depression hard
Or become who your thoughts or obsessions are
If you have any sadness
Then break it crushed
But take the push
All their crap make it flush
Because they're fake with us
I was just eating mac and cheese
Now I'm stacking geez
So stop acting please
A Black and a Chinese
Is a blackanese.
I want to go on a cruise
Send them home with a bruise
Now you know how they lose
Their scars mostly have blues.
You've got to be kidding me
Seriously you can't get rid of me
I come like a high fast ball
Because they're not hitting me
If they think they're splitting me
They must want double the trouble.
Want to cut it in half
I say, put it in graphs
About that work

But aren't loving the staff
This is annoying me
I don't see any loyalty
And it boils me
Could never let people spoil me
Going down a slippery road
Like it's oily
When we'll make it
Boy we'll see.
This concludes my rhyme
Hope you can include some time
Got to get these noobs in line
So they don't pass critical judgment.

Despair

This is the story of a brother and sister
Who had a hard life
Constantly watching both of their parents start fights.
The father consumed alcohol excessively
Would come home and start acting aggressively.
The most abuse for the boy he endured
Worst part is he didn't enjoy being poor.
Father always sent him to school
Physically hurt with a bruise
And the girl went through literally verbal abuse.
He was always picked on
Felt hurt but pretended
Could've fought back
But was afraid of being suspended
If he didn't take his life
Then his father is the reason it ended.
It was very few times the boy and the girl
Were enjoying the world.
They grew up in a home with no love
To fight the despair
Their friends expose them to drugs
But life isn't fair
It was all tears
Had to grow with no hugs.
The girl graduated
Now she's looking forward to college
Wasn't even congratulated
Or that fact wasn't acknowledged.
At this point she was like fuck it
I need to escape
Found a man twice her age

Was beaten and raped
Blamed herself for his rage
And asked why she was meeting that faith
Why she felt the despair.

I'm going to get back to the girl
Only not now
The boy didn't make it through school
He chose to drop out.
Would think of stuff he wouldn't miss
So he cut his wrists.
Wounds self-inflicted
To drug addicted
You could predict it.
It felt like the world
Was annoyed with you
No one would care to see
What the boy would do
Or even see things
From his point of view.
There was nothing he would do but cry
And had thoughts of suicide.
He felt lost with no hope
Which made him smoke dope
And even blow coke.
That day he was going to end his life
But he changed his mind
Looked at all the things that came with time
He overdosed on pills
To eliminate the pain inside
And told the doctors
Because no one feels it the same as mine.

Told god don't worry
That day has to come
So the next day he grabbed a gun
And didn't hesitate to have it done
His sister just had a son.
So she called to ask
When she could bring him
But the phone just kept ringing.
She never got an answer.

Just got the news of her brother's demise
After her brother's death
She felt like there was nothing left
One year later met a man her age
No longer feeling grief of her past
Because she moved past that page.
Finally found someone to love her
Doesn't make her suffer
And helps her be a good mother.
She sheds tears in the name of her sibling
But when she's with him she feels a different thing.
About to earn her degree
And said I deserve it for me
The things in her life
Are finally worth it to see
Then told the world
It's my turn to succeed.
About to start her career
Speaks to her brother
Because there's still part of him here.
Now she's about to get married
And thanks God for the new seed
He allowed her to carry.
Nine months later
Has a beautiful girl
Prettier than jewels and new pearls.
Now she's living very happily
And thanks God
For giving her a family.
No longer feeling despair
Her daughter's a breath of fresh air.
From here no more tears come after
Just cheers and laughter.
Getting passed the despair.

Dogs Rule

That is very deep
Every time I see a dog sleep
I want to get it
Go up to it and pet it
Give it a treat
Help every stray dog in the street
The ones left in the dark
And you can hear them bark
For a new journey in which they want to embark
Take them to the park.
Wait for it to poop
After the first loop.
And as you go home
Remember never to leave your dog alone
Give him a bone.
It has two souls his and yours
Gave you his heart and said this is yours.
And take it but don't break it.
I will be here to bring you cheers
In human and dog years.
But when dogs rule
They pick you
And when dogs drool
Then they lick you.
I'm man's best friend
Though I'm a dog
I don't pretend
We will be companions until the end.
Why do you think *dog* spelled backward is *god*.

East to West

I hope this message
Goes across the states
Before I get lost in fate
Lies is what it cost to hate
Watch me floss on dates.
Tell me where they stuck you at
If you're out of luck, who's that?
Drive safely, come save me
Do it bravely like you're in the Navy
It may be lately with the crazy ladies
That call me baby it's all gravy.
See you and me are what real is about
Speak until all your feelings are out
We're kneeling them down
Keep them sealed and don't shout
Banana peeling or sprout
Going to the ceiling's my rout
No stealing allowed
Not drug dealing I'm proud.
You know they get the misconception
I'm Colombian so they'll make a connection
Like I rigged the election
That's why I'm rushing
A lot of mistakes make the correction
They all want out but hate ejection
They might not like it so I get rejection
But they look in the mirror and see my reflection.
Just listen to music
Is it amusing

Miss it and lose it
Diss it and use it
Kiss it and bruise it
List it and choose it
This is where you sit.
I always write whatever's clever
Wishing I was around better weather
But it's forever never
So let me get a lever.
That way I can move it from east to west
And help to decrease the rest
I'll sit here and tease the best
And watch them become deceased from stress.

Every Day

How is your day going
In this life we've got to stay growing
With these words that I say knowing
My tears the wind away blowing.
Where do we go from here
Just move forward and show no fear
Listen to my words through both your ears.
I came with the scriptures
To paint you a picture
But the fame got them richer.
Call this rap or call it poetry
As long as you know it's me.
Write up a verse and flow with me.
Like water down a stream
You finally found your dreams
Feeling lonesome no one around it seems.
Good morning I slept with my eyes closed
And in the morning I rose
Then put away my clothes.
After I'll eat some breakfast
How did you start your day
They like to talk reckless
It's very dark and grey.
Reading this trying to study
But the weather got me dying my buddy
They don't see me crying who loves me.

They're right this sucks
Don't even have six bucks
When you achieve they say it's luck.
Adults can't act grown
Most with no backbone.
Another verse is what this is
Looking for a girl to make my misses.
I do it every day.

Feelings

When it came to you I felt overzealous
But you spoke to other fellows
Thinking I would be jealous.
But instead I was selfish because I wasn't willing to share
Know how it feels to know someone dearly is not aware
That you are there
The worst thing is they don't care
It makes you feel despair like life isn't fair.
With no desire to live you have so much to give
But no one to give it to
Trying to get rid of the pain that lives in you.
When you try to talk to her you get speechless
She takes your kindness for weakness
When you cry your nights sleepless
And start thinking I don't need this
But still try to reach this
Maybe I should take a different approach
Tired of dealing with the insults
Seems like being a bad guy brings me better results.
I'm sick of being nice and paying the price.
When someone else can get it for free
It was my mistake making them think
They were better than me
So I'm going to stop caring
And start letting them see
Women today don't want romance
They just want you to get with the program.
They don't want you to make them cry
And want to turn you down before you try
When all you want to do is wipe their eyes dry.
Only so it could feed their egos
They hurt you but they don't see you bleed though.
Don't complain when a man treats you bad

And constantly makes you sad.
You still think he needs a nice chick
He won't put his hands on you
But will mentally beat you down quick.
Maybe now you wished you hadn't turned me down
The lesson was hard but hopefully you learned it now
To him you weren't a queen he thought you didn't deserve a crown.
You could've been my goddess
I would've given you everything
Even if I was jobless.
But you wouldn't give me the time of day
I won't disturb you anymore
Maybe I'll resign today
If you can make your relationship better
I hope you find a way.
Don't get mad when I talk to your friends
If they need a companion I'm walking with them.
And you think it's okay
To say all men are the same
All they do is play games
But when we try to explain
Our mutual feelings you say that it's lame.
Talk about a double standard
Ask a woman about that and she won't answer
She can be your wellness or sickness like cancer.
Now I'm not saying it's okay
To make another girl suffer
Especially if you claim to love her
So I think of my sisters and mother.
Before I call a woman the B-word
I just want her to talk to me whenever she's hurt
Her pain can consume me first.
Probably won't get one like for this

A man will fight for a woman's love
But will she fight for his
I know a bunch who wouldn't
I could write a list.
Before I give my conclusion
In 2020 let's make a resolution.
To open our hearts
I'm hoping it starts
With this message that I wrote with these scars
Any girl talk to me and start reveling
What it is you're feeling
And I'll make you feel higher than the ceiling.
If you take the time to read this
I hope you don't think it's needless.
Because these are my feelings.

Fifty-Two Weeks

Every year has fifty-two weeks
Fifty-two weeks twelve months and four seasons
It starts in January
The winter time when it's freezing.
The new year started off blistering cold
When it's all over
Can't say I'll be missing the snow.
February is black history month
Meteorologists say
More inclement weather is to come
The Super Bowl is in this month
Other than that it isn't that fun.
Now in March it's the beginning of spring
When the sun and birds are out
And we're hearing them sing.
It's going to be a wonderful year in
Now that April is nearing
That's the rain month
Baseball fans are cheering.
And on 420 we see everyone blaze blunts
Can't wait until May comes.
I'm feeling the breeze
Enjoying the weather of fifty to sixty degrees
I'm out in shorts wearing a fleece.
Now that we're in June
I'm going to creep on the late night
Under a full moon
Summer arrives soon.
But who didn't see
That it would bring humidity.
June is over it's done
Since we're past the sixth month.
Let's take it into July

That's the seventh month
When a lot of events come.
On the second day I was born
Two days later we're celebrating some more.
Watching the sky light up
From the fireworks
And I am hurt.
On the twentieth is Colombia's independence
Hit up the parade with my best friends.
And August is the hottest month
And it's not a lot of fun
Unless the beach is at your reach.
Summer is almost over
And fall is getting closer.
Since we had all summer to act a fool
In September it's back to school.
Find some friends and have conversations
About what they did on vacations.
Just rekindle my summer was simple.
Now that the fall is here
Let's take it into October
The month I got sober
Watching the trees drop those leaves
So follow me into hollow's eve.
That's the only day we can wear a mask
Without being harassed.
What could I say
Don't know if you heard me.
November is worthy
Because I'm stuffing my face with turkey.
And I hope all the discounts come my way
On black Friday
Maybe I'll buy some apparel

In December we hear the Christmas carols.
We're seeing bright lights tonight.
Children singing songs for the holidays
And I've got to say the new year is on its way.
But until it's here spread some holiday cheer.
It's been fifty-two weeks.

From Within

Every time I sit in cars
With every line I'm hitting hard.
So I've got to come with the realness
To make them feel this
Go back to your nightmares
Fight the demons
But don't fight fair
When you're dreaming
Seems like he's right there
Hear him screaming.
Now wake your soul
Shake and roll
Break the hold
And take control
Walk the path
Lead the way
Talk and laugh
Need to say
What's on your mind
To put on this line.
I'm here for you homey
Never been a phony
A good friend only.
Now it's time I return the favor
Inhaling the fumes
When we burn the vapor
What we don't know now
We'll learn it later
Work hard and earn the paper
Have no concern for haters.
Think these are hard times
There could be more
Just like before

If we can only be sure
Then maybe we can see more
For sicknesses that we cure
But sometimes things happen for the best
Before you pour your heart out
Pull yourself together or we'll have a mess.
Just come out from within.

How It Is

You agree
We aren't free
Our origin tree.
Is what they took down
To write the books now.
But the mystery of history was miswritten
President mad because our words impact and his didn't
Now the last and final scripture is missing.
Dismantled civil rights organizations
That's why we still fight discrimination.
Native American, Black, and Hispanic groups gone
Like those foreign leaders they staged a coup on
Can't get a discount with a coupon.
The KKK still in existence
To perpetuate resistance
That's why the government won't dismiss them
They want to believe
In the so-called American dream
Dummies oblivious to reality
And arrogant screams.
But I don't hear you
Be careful snakes are near you
Yes America went to more war
To bring misery for poor
And say it's to open your doors.
So what's the latest
Another politician rapist
Thinking he's the greatest.
It is what it is how it is.

I'm A Seed

I'm not worried
About being buried.
Because I'm a seed
From the earth I feed
Only take what I need.
Don't bury me six feet deep
Bury me twelve
Don't worry it's well
In a hurry to hell.
So I will be like those who rose
And expose the foes.
They can put me beneath my grave
But they don't
Because we need the brave.
Bury me in a casket
I will break it like plastic.
Even in a mausoleum
Don't matter which god we pray to
At the end we got to see him
But not to be him.
Let reality collide with us
Because religion is dividing us.
See I believe in God's sun that shines
The light of the world that comes for mines
And the universe that runs with time
To the world from the universe from the line.
Let's worship the world
Rather than false idols
When it comes to being free
They're all rivals.
I don't mean to undermine anyone's beliefs
But religion causes solace and grief.

What I see in me
Is the worship of many deities.
God is an entity
But not one that was sent to me
Let's make an alliance with science.
And see what was really God given
All the necessities of life are not living
Burry me at night and I'll rise in the day.

Imagining

Well o well
You say LOL
But we fell in spells
Because we dwell in hell.
The things they're starting
Got kids marching
And others starving.
But they guess it's okay
I'll play the whole day
Score the goal
And give it my soul.
Go back and forth
Like ping-pong
Climbing buildings
Just like King Kong
Doing things wrong
Going to a melody when I sing songs
I haven't done it in a while
So they've bitten the style
This is written in tiles.
It's cool we speak a lot
Helping me keep the strength
No matter how weak I got.
They're fixing things
With soiled tools
Don't mean to annoy you fool
But yea O'Doyle rules
And this boy will drool
Whenever he's seeing food
Forgive me if I'm being rude.
It's just a figment of my imagination.

In God They Trust

Separate god from politics
But politicians are very similar
To those who preach god and religion
To make false promises
Is their job and their mission.
During their campaigns
They speak with deception
Then on the night of elections
They expect us to make a selection.
So when they ask me to vote
I reply with one word *nope*
They're the ones leaving us broke
Down with no hope
And back against the ropes.
The real issues aren't acknowledged
Presidents are elected
By the electoral college.
Now we're all being held hostage.
By a system
Which relies on us voting
To see more bombs exploding.
The banks are known
To snatch our homes
And the government
To tap our phones.
Airliners getting lost off the coast of Asia
Going to China from Malaysia
And when they try to explain
You can see signs of aphasia
They can infiltrate nations
But have no explanation

When classmates are shooting themselves up
With no hesitation.
We must check our peripherals
And see all the crap
From the Conservatives and Liberals.
In God they trust.

Now don't get me started on religion
Because it was only meant for division.
And control of one's soul.
They attempt to condemn you.
Like if you give birth
Your child just came to this earth
It's like sin comes with him
He has it within.
Yet they tell you
Only God can help you
But if you don't believe in him
You're destined for eternal darkness and hell too.
Well, where was God on nine eleven
He was doing fine in heaven.
There were lives so many took
Where was God for Sandy Hook
He just sat there and he looked.
Send your kids to Catholic schools
And the priests are molesting your sons
At the same time the church is collecting your funds.
The bible was written by man
And it was hidden by plans
Never to give in thy hands.
The so-called Word of God
Put into commandments
Meant to tell you what to do
Why do you think they call them commandments.
Pay for communion and confirmation
They sold us a lie
December 25 is not the birth of Jesus
They told us a lie.
In God they trust.

In My World

In my world
Everything wouldn't be perfect
But living life would be worth it.
There wouldn't be innocent dying
And children crying
Or politicians lying.
Everyone would eat
There wouldn't be bums in the street.
We wouldn't have greed
Only take what we need.
In my world everyone would own property
And there wouldn't be poverty.
There wouldn't be such thing as hunger
And every day would be summer.
There wouldn't be wars
Or meaningless reasons to die for.
There wouldn't be religious persecution
And people being put to death by execution
It would only be world evolution
Everything would have a peaceful solution
And we wouldn't have pollution.
We wouldn't have suicides
Or people being euthanized
Everything would be purified.
My world would be an inner sanctum
Where rappers would actually have to be good
In order to go platinum.
Cops wouldn't harass in the street
And cats in the street
Wouldn't be packing the heat.
Weed would be legal
And there would be no need to be evil.
We would all have high-paying jobs

And worship the same gods.
To revive us
Religion wouldn't divide us.
In this world of mine
We would respect nature
Show everyone love except haters
Everyone would be real they'd detect fakers.
My world would be a wonderful place
Where we wouldn't look at one another's face
In disgrace for their race
All that would be erased.
Gangbangers wouldn't be doing shoot-outs
When they're driving by
We wouldn't ask mothers why you cry
And hear the reply
Because my child just died
Instead we would fight together side by side.
In my world there wouldn't be liars
Boys would be loyal to girls
And they would both be enjoying the world.
And women would be loyal to the end
Fathers would raise their kids
And turn their boys up into men.
In my world there wouldn't be promiscuity
Or animal cruelty
We wouldn't be divided it'll only be unity
It would be me and you
Because there is no I in you and me.
We would have different ways or answers
There wouldn't be such thing as AIDS or cancer.
People wouldn't be popping pills by prescription
And end up with a real drug addiction
Tell me about your world or give a description.

Because I'm letting you read what I say about mines
A world where children are playing outside.
Everything is real
Athletes aren't using drugs
To enhance their performance
Then get million-dollar endorsements
And we're not being told what to do
By government enforcements
This is my world friend.

In the Year of Our Lord

In the year of our Lord
A boy named Jayden was born
And on that day
I knew we would take the world by storm
It was a blessing of some form
When you get old enough to understand
The words from this man
You'll learn to love the land.
And be kind but don't be blind
Always follow the signs.
Be nice to your mom and dad
Because they're the ones to hold you and console you
When you're sad
Matter fact after that

Just know I'll always have your back.
When people be hating on Jayden.
It's because they're some jealous fellows.
What they fail to tell us
Is that this is your first year
To bring in the new year
Thanks for the new cheers
You've brought through here.
When it's all over
I'm going to show you some cool stuff
When you get older now that I'm sober
I have no need to look over my shoulder.
Just stay strong and play on
When you feel like the day's long.
Always love nature
And everything good will come later.
Every time I carried you
You loved taking my hat
You'll probably grow up to be hating my hats.
Or you will take after your mom
And be very studious
To prepare for a world that's dubious.
The day you were born I was very hyper
Just glad I didn't have to change your diaper.
And your uncle
Will show you love by the bundles
Remember to always stay humble
And you'll be held when you stumble.
Even though you couldn't walk and couldn't talk
I see where you're going
And know what you say

Where are you going today.
Just move forward and look toward a new day.
Maybe not now or later
But some day you'll thank me
When you get older
We'll go to the Bronx and watch the Yankees.
Then we'll play soccer
And you'll be so good it'll be a shocker
Remember holding your head
And you crying when you wanted to be fed
Didn't let your mom go to sleep
Wanted to stay up and play instead.
Learned to crawl upstairs
Because you were curious
As to what's up there.
Just know we'll always love you
Because you're a gift from the gods.

In the Year of Our Lord (Part 2)

In the year of our lord
A boy named Jayden was born
And on that day
Well hey what could I say
All you want to do is play.
Don't want to sleep don't want to eat
But you're still the cutest boy
Thank you for bringing us the newest joy
You're happy with the fewest toys
Because running around is what you enjoy
Start crying when you're feeling too annoyed.
So look at what this is
Baby boy give me kisses
The one my heart always misses.

So yes, you won't guess.
It's your uncle again
Thank you for being my humblest friend
With you the struggles will end
You were lovable then
And you're more adorable now.
You can almost speak
I heard you said a new word last week.
Be nice to your mom and dad
Even when your mood is on the bad.
Take advantage of all the opportunities
Your palm will have
I love you baby nephew
Always be glad to help you.
As I write this I hope you like this.
You're not old enough to read yet
I tell you with no regrets
Thanks to you for the happiness we get
I want it to start over press reset.
You're God's gift to the earth
Jayden this is your birth
Everything life is worth.
Your day is the nineteenth
Treat your uncles and grandma nicely
And see who they might be.
So many things you will soon create
You're just turning two
Which is why me and you relate.
I see you growing very purely
Slowly but surely
But as you grow
Don't forget to glow

Take life slow
Don't be in a rush
Go pee in a bush.
Climb trees hop fences
Remember who your true friend is
Enjoy your childhood
It's priceless, not endless.
Play outside in the playground
And get dirty
Show them you're worthy
Baby boy I got to go
But I love you a lot, you know
This is real life, not a show.
I'll see you soon.

In the Year of Our Lord (Part 3)

In the year of our Lord
A boy named Jayden was born.
And on that day
You would go away
About to take your first trip
You have to poop
Let the worst rip
Today is your birthday
I'm sad because you won't be here on Thursday
Bring back photos who you're with
When you get back
I already packed your gift
Go there and wreak havoc
Whatever you seek grab it
Baby boy I'm going to miss you
The reason for our happiness is you
I'm going to be here waiting for Jayden.

Juliette

In the year of our Lord
A girl named Juliette was born.
And on that day
Which is in May.
You were born a girl
To adorn the world
Like a form of pearl
Or a storm that swirls.
Going into your fifth month
Drinking your milk
Until your bottle is with none.
And you look so pretty in pink
That the entire city will think.
It's a beacon of light
Baby girl you're a freaking delight
I can't wait until you speak and you write
You and Jayden on the weekends will fight.

Now it's getting more cold
Things you'll understand
When you're old
You're a goddess
That's what was foretold.
As I hear you breathing
I see you teething.
You're a happy girl who hardly cries
Without you the family partly dies.
Now that you crawl
Give me a hug
But you'd rather sprawl
All on the rug.
In your first year
You've got a verse here
I love you, baby girl.

L.I.F.E. (Lost Internally For Eternity)

Now how can I find my way out
Not satisfied with how things are going
Or the way they'll play out.
Not knowing the things that are glowing.
Are the ones that burn me
Life is a long journey
And it concerns me.
Because I've been lost internally for eternity
No one felt they could turn to me
So alone is how I learned to be.
And end up lost inside forever
Don't know what it costs to try for better
In each line across in my whole letter.
The day I arrived on this planet
Never took it for granted
From the clouds haven't landed.
Now I'm paying for the mistakes of the past
Paying for them
Like they're taking my cash
The debt is never ending
Am I making it last
When my life is on crutches
I'm breaking the cast
Trying to get my feet wet
The lake's in a flask
Enjoy yourself
Have some cake and a blast.
Where am I headed
Was never given enough credit
It's not about what's said
But who said it.
Create an opportunity
And go get it

With a small ego
Because I never fed it
It felt like things were going to blow up
Like I was running from bombs
I remained humble and calm
Never with a gun in my palm
Only with a son and a mom
When you come I'll be gone.
Conflict I'm likelier to ignore
I choose to write rather than fight
Because the pen is mightier than the sword.
Wish I could disappear
Leave here with no fear
Hoping God is near
When your life is smeared.
Don't know where to find the strength
To give it your time and length
Just went from nine to tenth.
Until they make me be
Something I don't want to be
And I make them see
Something eventually they're going to see.
Now if actions speak louder than words
Then why do people treat you
Based on what they heard.
The world is a court
Where everybody's a judge
Regret of some sort
The words won't make you budge
Life is good, but it's short
To always stay with a grudge
If they take this as sport
Then I'm touched by a nudge

Hold down the fort
After you were just smudged.
If I said something that offended you
It's called freedom of speech
Don't take it like it was intended to
Just a goal I need them to reach
What they all pretend to do
Is lead them and teach.
Inside feeling misguided
No one is straight
Everyone now is sided
Is it too late.
For me to see the end
Or is my life free to lend
Is God my enemy or is he a friend.
I'm Lost Internally for Eternity
But that's LIFE.

Like It or Not

Now their term has passed
I've learned at last
How to earn the cash
I'll burn the trash
And watch it turn to ash
Their lane just confirmed a crash.
But it wasn't an accident
Now I'm smoking sacks with them
So watch my pack extend.
Just increased
The size of my circle
And released
All of my verbals
They're deceased
I'm smoking the purple
The way I'm pleased
Is consuming the herbal
Their plans were ceased
For moving like turtles.
Have a good day at work
Make sure you pay a perp
And what you say won't slur
Got to remember to stay alert
You don't need to pray in church
On the bed you're laying hurt
Thinking when you played in dirt.
Those times are missed
No one writes rhymes like this.
Hopefully we can speak
Sometime this week
About all we seek
But for now I'll peek
Kiss the cheeks
Like mafiosos do.

L.M.A.O. (Let's Make America Ours)

No, this is not a battle this is more
Like a civil war
Why did they conquer our land for.
Now I understand more.
Rather than see one another separate by races
Let's just focus and get to our places
The path was set by the traces
Left from our ancestors
This land was stolen
That's our power they're holding
The truth is unfolding
Knocking down the pins like bowling
Well we keep rolling.
All the messages I hope you heard them
I'm telling you about the men
Behind the curtain
Who run things for certain.
All while we're working
In a hospital we can't get hurt in.
We take losses
Like we don't notice
While the bosses
Only focus
On getting rid of you
But won't care what it did to you
Or if you have a kid in school.
All they care about is saving money
While we're the economic slaves for money.
People are more hungry
Than a little kid
In a poor country
And I don't know what's up
With all these acts of indignation

Toward immigration in this nation.
But we never heard them complain
When undocumented workers
Were brought here in chains.
So I'm going to write the mean bars
That'll hit the fiends hard
And even turn them to retards
My people live illegal
Because they're immigrants without a green card.
See America was one giant strip
From Canada to the South American tip
Before they came over on ships
And Africans took a trip
To get hit with a whip.
Conquered the continent
Dropping a bomb again
The world is on the end
Don't send your kids to prom with friends.
They might not come back
From the schools where the guns at
To the field where they run track
Thanks to a system that's done that
Your kid went in smart
And came out dumb-whacked.
They want to arm a teacher
And harm a creature.
Everything in crises
Residents paying the prices
While they're hooked on devices
Thinking it's where real advice is
So now this is where ice is
Get cut in dices
For being the nicest.

Republicans and Democrats
Powers of axis
Getting our taxes.
Only for profit
We should get off it.
That's why we won't evolve
But instead dissolve
Through a door that revolves
If money's not involved
Then problems don't get solved.
So I'm going to say it
With no interruptions
As long as there's money
We'll have corruption
Without it a truth eruption
A world in destruction.
Religion and government conjunction
A society that can't function.
By the system they were allowed and did it
That's why it's misbegotten
It's another foul committed
Democracy is forgotten
Let's come to rid it
Because this is rotten.
Until it's clean in
They keep doing things
With no meaning
In this reality we're dreaming.

Be careful, things we're perceiving
Very much could be deceiving
Only give back what we're receiving
Who's the one to believe in
Follow me as I'm leaving.
This country was founded on lies
Hear screaming soldiers sounds as they die
Take a look deep down in my eyes
Will anyone be around when I cry
The leaders are just clowns wearing ties
Even small towns getting dry
Lift our pounds when we try.
Let's make America ours again.

Meant to Be

What's meant to be
Was sent to me.
If it finds its way
Hopefully, it's on this day.
Most definitely, inevitably
If it's destined to be
Thankfully, you're not resting in peace.
Look at the world we made
We'll regret it
When we're at the pearly gates.
Let's just love the earth
Because it's where we came from birth.
When we love not hate her
She's our mother nature.
Let's stop shooting and stop polluting
What are we doing
The world is ruined
Product of us looting.
When you see those natural catastrophes
It's because we annoyed her
And we just destroyed her.
So she causes another earthquake
And we feel the wrath of mother earth shake.
Where has this world been sent
Soon to arrive at the end.

Let's have more love as humanity
So we can do what we want to do happily
Only time we help one another
Is when we're going through tragedy
It's time we use a new strategy.
If we really want to live in peace
Then let's not let the clips release
And see some kids deceased
We should be uniting
Rather than effing fighting.
Pardon my French
But the real players in this game
Are on the bench.
Which would explain why I'm sitting.

Men Don't Cry

They say men don't cry
Well who told you that lie
When I'm sad I can't keep my eyes dry
So I've got to get high
And think about this life
That's been passing me by.
Because there were times
When life got the best of me
That's how I knew
I couldn't make my own destiny.
Things I've been around and seen
Got me kind of nervous
Asking myself in this life what is my purpose
Wish I can put myself six feet beneath the earth's surface
Because being in this earth is
Kind of worthless.
It feels like the world is gunning for me
And the envious are coming for me
You know the kind of pain and shame.
That it put on me.
At nights I'd go to sleep
And my dreams and nightmares
Would come back to haunt me
It's like the devil was talking to me
He was trying to taunt me.
Then I woke up one morning and wondered
Should I live this day
Or put myself six feet under.
It's like where do I go
There's no place for me.
I put my past behind me
And my mistakes over
Every time I stayed sober

It's like heaven doesn't want me
And hell is afraid I'm going to take over.
Heard people out there
Saying Edwin has issues
But they would never trade their lives
To put themselves in his shoes
Or hand him some tissues.
To wipe his tears
When he cried inside
Only way out was to fight his fears
When he died inside.
They messed with me
Until I had to blow them out
But I'm knowing now
I'm going down.
A path
At which I can't follow
But before I go with my eyes closed.
Let my life flash before my eyes
Before I die.
So I can live to regret it
Or forgive and forget it.
Perhaps on this I'm expected
To be dissed and neglected
But missed and respected
If you think men don't cry.

Modern-Day Poetry

This is the manifest
And now they have a test
Duck or grab a vest
Make sure you have the best
So you can strap your chest.
With the guns they bring
Too dumb to think
Who's running in
You've begun to spin
I heard it's cold out
But that's just hearsay
Look out the window it's a clear day
Drive slow if you're in a deer's way
If the game is here play
If you're near stay.
I'll have my mind awake ears
The modern-day Shakespeare
Watch how quickly I break jeers
Scary thing I take fear
Come look at what I make here
Chicken steak beer
Artificial fake cheers
I make the ground shake near
Drink water from a lake deer.

I just wrote them a sample
That they couldn't handle
Read it and start with the scandals
They'll get blown out like candles
After they're dismantled.
From this angle
But at first it's won
And the worst will come
After the verse is done.
You just read modern-day poetry.

Never Forget

Never forget about those
Who stayed loyal
Through the bad times when you rose
Thank you for staying by my side
Unlike the rest
So I want to share my success
With those who helped me
Become the best
I'm not trying to hold myself on a high pedestal
But at the same time I'm not that terrible.
Don't blame me
When I want to get it all
With a goddess that the heavens call.
Something a little further than far
Do you know where you are.
You need to be lost
To find your own way
Try to make it home
Even if it takes the whole day.
Find a significant other
That's worth the keep
In a place of peace
While you sleep
And then awake
Before you break.
Never forget

New Era

We're the ancestors
To plant the seeds tonight
This is what they need all right
So if you read I write
The weed I light
Just bleed and fight
A new breed in sight
To lead with might.
And I follow through
With my Spanish troops
Now this man is duped
Goddamn I'm pooped
Roam the land in loops
But understand the truth.
This is our second life
From a previous era
Without devious terror
And the media's errors.
Even the best corrected
And resurrected
Blessed respected
A mess expected.
Who's going to clean up
No more green bucks
Everyone is lean cut
Everything you've seen shut
In reality your dreams put.

See you in another earth
Thank you Mother Earth
Go to love the earth
Never let you suffer earth
Maybe in another birth
They'll understand how much you're worth
In a new era.

Objective

I'm going to be selective
To achieve my objective.
When I'm doing this mission
These words I shoot with precision
So hurry up and choose a decision.
Words beneath graves they're full of diggers
But they'd rather pull the trigger
Can't get to my head because my skull is bigger.
Some of them come with men
Guns and friends run and sent
From the end.
They want to awake the sleeping giant
Look at me and peep a tyrant
With their words they keep on lying
Won't even know they're asleep and dying
Everything is cheap they're buying
And they're still deep denying
From the tip I'll take a leap I'm flying.
With a body so skinny
They say I'm depleted
Can't see me I'm deleted
How many of them conceited
Sickness untreated
Write it and read it
Like if you need it.

People Who Hate

So right we can't hate and attract
Only create and adapt.
Rather than talk about change
Let's just do it first
For love of the universe
Pay attention to the message
When I go through this verse.
Since the beginning we've been haunted
Worked hard for what we wanted
But got our rear end
With a foot print on it.
A case of divide and conquer
Is more like conquer and divide
There's a monster on my side
Come on in and just hide.
Those still holding their heads high
After all the miserable times they had
They separated us with invisible lines on maps.
The truth is, we're all one and the same
That's how everyone comes in the game
Make way and assist
For those who want to run in your lane.
I'm trying to let the ladies and fellows see
There wouldn't be hate without jealousy
Rather than envy me
You should be helping me
But instead you're telling me
You were alone
When you caught a felony
That's the reason you point a gun
And say give up everything as you yell at me
If we want to make change well let's see
Hopefully I can aid with that in this melody.

The world is only as messed up
As the humans who inhabit it
We have an opportunity for change
But we're not grabbing it.
Because it's easier'
To leave things the same
It's mind control
Not preaching here
Just thought it's time you know
Let's wake up and see.

Perpetual Verbals

Listen to the words I say when I speak
Every single day of the week
Following the way that I seek
And I'll stay on my peek
Red displayed on my cheeks.
When I play in the street
I'll lay in the heat
Start to pray when I eat.
And pay all it costs
When my phone rings
It means they called the boss.
To make it out the hole
Because when you fall you're lost
But they rather ball and floss.
Everything coming out is perennial
So make way for the millennials.
What they've done is not for unity
But if you see an opportunity.
Then go and grab it
Just like you hold a habit
I prefer laptops
Because you can't fold a tablet.
I'll hit the sweet spot
Give you a meal
So you can eat hot.
Hearing people singing carols
As I'm bringing barrels
With real news things from heralds.

They don't know what I've been about
Man, I'll go in and out
Then win the bout
Let's begin to shout
If they only want half
Go get a cutter
Like it's your bread and butter
Can't understand what they said they stutter
With this I'll think ahead
Write it in ink or led
But now I'm on the brink of dead.

Question Everything

Politicians I trust none
Because those who run
Want to take your guns
Along with your rights one by one
And then some.
Like the right to bear arms
Caused very rare harm.
It's in the constitution
Taking it away is not the solution.
But force us to obey tax laws
Written by bankers
Who invade nations steal resources for profit
Financial gangsters
We're asking the wrong people
It's why we don't find answers.
All these crimes reported about Hispanics is so wild
Hope you know it's only meant to profile.
And MS-13 doesn't help the cause
But you can't tell you're lost
After all the hell you crossed
Got a very big well applause.
Now what is up with this Hispanic illegal
Got away with rape
Giving a bad name to our people
Should've got shot but escaped.
There's good and bad in every race
That's something I know and see
So before we talk about immigrants
Let's go overseas.
With that kid who plays ball
Who is not so small.
Got a free trip to China
Because he's God-gifted

And barely got a slap on the wrist
After he shoplifted
While one who does it out of necessity
Gets knocked with it
And told they should've not did it.
Let's not forget the Rio Olympics
The US team from swimming
And the vandalization
They were committing
At that gas station
And got banned from that nation
Let's get more abroad
And talk about corporate greed
And all the war it brought.
Or how about the first illegal immigrants
Who came around
Thought they were innocent
Until they killed the browns.
With these words I'll paint
Nobody is a saint
Not saying my race doesn't have taint.
But we don't want money or power
Just what's rightfully ours
Putting in work at nights full of hours.
Look at what we're doing
Saying I'm this I'm that
When we're all human
I don't talk about God
Because I never knew him
Let's come together and question everything.

Real-Life Fiction

I hope they enjoy my verses
And don't think they're worthless
Bury them under the surface
After they serve you like customer service
So exclusive they won't believe you heard this
I could drop F-bombs and other curses.
Coming out with new treats
How many people can you seat
For dinner I might do meat
It's up to me to eat
In and out and through streets.
This is how we roll
Missed this now we're old
Kisses how she's told.
Through time we went and came back
Got our minds on the same track.
Since I was a little seed
I kept on yapping
From here to Italy
We hear them clapping
Any way literally
We make it happen
They want to cripple me
Since we keep scrapping
And then it'll be
Where I'm trapped in.
I'm like a fire
Burning old spots
When I retire
I'll be turning so hot
Got what's required
Learning don't stop.
Ready to cash in

Until I see lights flashing.
In the surface feel the friction
This is real life fiction.
Trying to wait
For it to become late
On today's date.
What are you doing up
People running their lips
Just glue them shut
Feel the message going through your gut
It's the salt in your wound and cut
Praying to soon for luck
You might be doomed and tucked
Don't forget to shoot and duck
Human food is yuck.
On Christmas eve
The story of the winter solstice
Is misbelieved
Now tell me is this the grieve
I'll give you another hand wrist and sleeve.
How pretty they light up trees
More than December
Put a fight up please
Now you're a member.
The entire world is a wild fire
Every mother, father, and child's tired
So they're quick to bite a style dire.
If they don't have balls
I'll hand them a sack
Trump took his anxiety meds
For Hispanic attacks
Now it's tragic and whack
Be careful his magic is black

Yes the havoc is back
Putting hammocks on tracks.
To run them over with a train
Coming sober with the pain
With the weight of the world
On my shoulders and my brain
The poison feels colder in your veins.
Like the blood that flows
And the flood that goes.
It'll eventually get somewhere
It feels like life was set unfair.
It's like nope you can't win
No matter how righteous we live
Every man sins
In this dirt put your hands in
Because even the devil was an angel
And heaven banned him
But you got to hold your own
And always stand slim.
Take life slowly with no beef
And no grief.
Really early make their troops retire
Only our size boots required
Jumping through hoops of fire
We're doing loops with tires.
In the morning hear the birds chirp
Some wisdom words heard.
What do you have planned for the day
I can't stand what they say
They could land in my way
But they can't cause they stay
Break their hands when they play.

Everything in this mind is me
They're all to blind to see.
Because they don't have the will to see
These accomplishments to fulfill with me
So we can travel together
Go through battle whenever
Trapped in shackles forever.
To where they send you
Until they end you.
In real life or fiction.

Reality Speaks

Donald Trump can kiss my hump
After I take a dump on that chump
I'd rather have as president
Someone from the slums maybe a bum
I can see him doing bumps
At the oval office
How the hell did he get control of all this.
It's a shame
I don't know what kind of name
I should call this
What was it that we all missed
Money and power
Is why they switch
He is only in office
So he can stay rich
Those who claim he would do a lot for your nation
Don't forget he's a businessman and America's a corporation.
So it makes sense
While he makes millions
On America's investments
That's why everyone detests him
And they all want to test him.
That hypocrite shouldn't speak though
He hesitated to send aid to Puerto Rico
It took him almost a week bro.
But you know what thanks
Just like us
They're in debt to the banks

And Wall Street
While we're slaves
And they all eat
We can all change this
So reach out and call me
They want to change things falsely.
Now everything
Keeps getting stranger and stranger
Never before in history
Have our rights been in danger
That's it, I'm done
Hope you enjoy it
And have fun.
When reality speaks.

Rich at Heart

I would be rich
With only one piece of bread
A roof with water leaking over my head
Just a room and a bed
To let you know what I said.
See I could be poor
Sleep on a floor
If I have you what I want more.
Might not have money to eat
But will never let us sleep on the street
Stand on our own feet.
Because we're all that we need.
Have something more than money—values
Whenever I have you
The most valuable things in life
Is trust dignity and self respect
I'm just grateful for the help I get.
I tip my hat to those who support a family
Not financially stable
But do it any way they're able
To put bread on the table.
The inner you is capable
Of being unbreakable
So when we think we have it bad.
Let's think first
There're others who are
And been worst
Dying of hunger and thirst.
Still manage to survive
A real man until I die.

Never give up on your family
Because without money
You can live happily
Let me give you all I have in me.
The real riches come from nature
Not the ring you gave her
But everything it made her
The one that saved her.
I'm not kidding
The real rich is from within.
Just be rich at heart.

Seven Days

It's Monday the beginning of the week
Not looking forward toward going to work
Because I'm still hungover and hurt
But I can't bang out I should sober up first.
I can't wait for this day to finish.
Hoping for a new day now it's Tuesday
That's the day of the god of war
Right before hump day
I've got to keep moving ahead
I'm stuck on one way.
It's a good day to get it in at the gym.
How little did I see
We're on to Wednesday
That's the middle of the week
But it's a sunny day
The sun will hit you with the heat.
All the days passed way fast
But I didn't think that they'd last.
Since we're passed the third day
Let's take it into Thursday.
That's day number four
The day of the god of thunder, Thor.
It's a beautiful day
I should ride my bike
The moon is shining the stars are out
It's perfect for a drive tonight.
We're almost at the end of the week.
Next is Friday, that's my day, it's been five days.
But it came way late
That's okay because it's a pay date.
Just got out of work
Everything is boring now
Maybe later I'll take a shorty out.

I have direct deposit
So my cash I got it
Now I got money to stuff my pockets.
Trying to find something to do
But no one is out so I'm guzzling brew
Just getting drunk with a crew.
It's past midnight.
And today is Saturday
That's the day that the children have to play
Now I'm glad to say.
That I know from the start
I want to take a girl
For a stroll in the park.
Then at night hit up my boy
And be like, let's party, dude
I want to hit up a bar with you.
Until 4:00 a.m. now it's Sunday
You should come to my barbecue
It's going to be at my backyard come through.
Call my friends and see where they're at
Come by, we can eat, drink, and play catch.
If not just spend time with the family
Can't drink too much
But I drank them so rapidly.
Damn this really sucks.
Looking ahead to the new week
Because I'm going to do me
Tomorrow I'm back at it again.

Some People will Never Get You

Some people will never get you
They'll just give up on you and forget you
Set up traps where step through
You want to quit, but your strength won't let you
How can they get you.
When they don't even get themselves
Do things they regret themselves.
I've been lost internally for eternity
But that's life.
When it comes for a favor they turn to me
The fire inside is burning me
Now I've learned to see
That it's the world versus me.
Might say something you don't like
So you look at me differently
Criticize and make judgments instantly.
Only look at the sins in me since it's me.
If you're free of sin throw the first stone
Angry because you come from the worst home.
We all have demons inside
Which we battle
When we dream and we cried
We run but it seems we can't hide.
That's why I cherish those
Who helped me when I rose
Even after the truth exposed
Couldn't have me disposed.

The ones who lifted my soul
Were blessed and gifted then told
To not resist and then fold
Or they will only exist in a hole
In this world we live, it's so cold
Want to make it to the end
You've got to love it
We're already at the beginning of it
Look at the signs.

Speak Your Mind

Hell yea speaking your mind
Might get you beat from behind
These people aren't reading the lines
And I don't need to be kind
The truth is what you don't see cause you're blind.
Feel me this is going to be real deep.
In a world so cold but we're burning
People rather be entertained rather than learning
In this day and age it's hard to determine.
What's real what's not
What's ill what's hot.
After twenty nineteen
All these many times seem.
Like since we were born we've never been free
So wake up because this is forever to see.
Little by little we're losing our rights
But people think it's necessary
Rather than choosing to fight.
And the ones on the top love it
They got the public controlled like puppets
When you open your mouth they want you to shut it.
We need permission even to go fishing
And have to ask to collect rainwater
But just sign a paper to be deployed
And have millions slaughtered
They don't care if it's your son or daughter.
They hit them off with a nice bonus
To make them lose focus
So where are we now
Take a look around
We've got a president who's dumb
I'm talking about that chump
Who's going to suck the life out of this country

Until there's nothing left but a crumb.
Let him build a wall in his backyard
So the neighbors won't have to look at that ugly fat lard
Now we're two decades into the millennium
Still fighting terrorism
Sending soldiers to kill and be killed
And show it as heroism
Islam is not the problem
It's the corrupt bankers, politicians, corporations
And the greed they have in common.
It might piss some people off the things I say
Of course before you get fooled one more day.
Ask yourselves what's the source
Before we find cause to fight wars.
Let's fight for the poor.
There's some reality for you all

Tables Have Turned

I'm in my pajamas
They want to slam us
Time to unhand us
They really can't stand us.
It's the newest clan
Tell me who's your man
Left or right
Choose your hand
It's death tonight
Lose your land
A theft in sight
On news with bands
Each breath is light
In my shoes I stand.
Up very, very tall
If you believe in God
I'm from where he calls
I tend to grieve a lot
It's a scary fall
Greed in the sleeves they got
Now I'm sharing all.
Yeah, I'm back on my game
I attack without shame
I'll crack them the same
Just rack what I gain
And whack is their name
In a shack when it rains
I'm stacking the fame
They're acting so lame
White and Black when I aim.

Can't say I'm a racist
They're scared when they face this
For not knowing where their place is
Undetectable, they can't trace this
Written in ink can't erase this
Don't let it rip, you can't replace this.

The Day After

It's the day after
The only thing I could say
Is have a good day
Forget the hood way.
So just follow me
Now that I'm allowed to be
Any character
Life is a bitch
But don't be mad at her
Just confront her
And be the baddest sir
Even if you're feeling sad and hurt.
Wish I was growing some weed
While I'm going to sleep
I'm flowing to deep
I'm knowing your peeps
And I'm showing those creeps
That I'm blowing those beeps
Approach it slow in those leaps
Stay on the low and don't keep.
On falling in a rush down
Wondering when you will touch ground
Don't know too much now
Words that'll have you touched wow.
In the day after.

The Rise

Get that wealth
And share with bosses
Or get prepared for losses
Devilish scared of crosses
You don't care then toss this
When they stare I floss this.
Don't listen to what they say
Tomorrow is payday.
I would have to fight myself
To beat the winner
Make sure you eat some dinner
Before you become in the street a sinner
Mother earth is cold no heat is in her
Go away in completely glimmer.
Of light into the night
Winning the fight
From here I'll be surprising
And appear from the horizon
Afraid because we're the ones uprising
Living in fear
Now they're despising
They'll all be whack
You missed my call
Don't forget to call me back
So we can get on the rise.

Treatable Cause

Dems got it signed
On the dotted line
But not in time
It's okay if you shot the nine
Or if you drop a rhyme.
But be dammed if you defend yourself
Approve medications that pretend to help
But only end your health
Name to complicated to pronounce
With the pen they spelled
A fat ass check when they sell.
The health system is like everything else
They just treat it
Force medications down your throats
Convinced that you need it.
Same as laws
When you get knocked
You hear an applause
But life just paused
Can't get rid of the problem
So they treat the cause.
Own a gun
Or get hit
With stones to run
Life is where your home is done
Now they're grown and dumb
I've on my own begun.
On this treatable cause.

Trust No One

Why is it
Anyone of the four seasons
I see more treason for no reason.
If you're banking on luck
Tell me your plans
I've got to make it on my own
No one to help me advance
In high school
I used to go by myself to the dance
Kind of sad isn't it
Because I fell in a trance
Got an opportunity
Trying to excel with this chance.
Look in your friend's eyes
Now you're staring at death
Just want to put you beneath
Like they're scared of your breath
They don't want you to breathe.
Don't know if you heard me
The same ones on your side
Will be doing you dirty
Don't let anything slide
Your girl and him getting flirty
They all promised and lied
Who couldn't hurt me
After I died.
Now the days are strange
Because the ways have changed
No longer stay in range.
But I remain kind and calm
Until my mind is gone
And maybe that time is on.
Me and the heavens
We've got alliance

You can't figure it out
It's not rocket science
They can take me out
But not in silence
Now I'm hearing
The coppers siren
Like they shot a tyrant
But even that
Won't stop the violence.
Want to end me for a dollar
When I'll lend you two
No one by your side now
Your friend is who?
Predict your own death
And the end is true
Enemy knocking at your door
Like a landlord when rent is due.
Is his life worthy to take
See you hurt for his sake.
If you want to pull the trigger, let's go
This can be hazardous like cigarette smoke
But instead it's meant for the sick to get hope
Saw someone I didn't like, but I didn't step though
Looked like a peaceful man, and I live to rep those.
Could've ended him
Over some nonsense
But I don't want to live with that
On my conscience.
Because I'm trying to fix the problem
Not be the source
So of course
I have to show remorse
Not take a life by force

In life trust no one.
People got me paranoid
Someone let me have a roid
Because I am annoyed.
With all these thoughts
I might black out
What my elders taught
I'll bring it back now
The things you sought
They were lacked now
The things you bought
Never packed now.
Trying to be nice but I'm lost
And I can't pay the price that it cost
Bad luck with the dice that you tossed.
Now you're impetuous
They'll tell you where to aim
But only to let you miss
I'm honestly not sure
If I can get through this.
Let the world criticize me
No one prepared me
And they think I'm insane, just barely
My own thoughts would scare me
If they knew what went through my head
They wouldn't dare me
So they misjudge me
And treat me unfairly.
Because I have to fight the media
When I give you more facts
Than encyclopedias
If I had any hate in my blood
It would be a sickness like anemia.

Unheard Of

I write about things that are random
Maybe if I write about DE's and magnums
Then I'll have an album
That might just go platinum
Girls think I'm handsome
I made it and got fouled and one.
Go out with a bang
Made your voice
Heard so loud when you sang.
Now on some real shit
That's too complicated to deal with
Their show I'm going to steal it
And expose it before they seal it
The truth concealed quick
But I'm here to reveal bits
Of how it makes me feel sick.
The NRA stands for never resolves anything
Putting money in the pockets of politicians
Pulling many strings.
There were seventeen dead
Now in a heavenly bed
Jesus rested on the seventh we said.
Now we've got kids making noise
To hear their voice
While they still have a choice.
What happened in Florida
Got them asking if the door is shut
But informed people know more is up
And yes it sure is nuts.

Now on to the wall
Make it very tall
The harder the fall
Who're they going to call.
To rebuild it
Give them a guilt trip
On a paper that will rip
Walk straight and still slip
Shoot guns with filled clips.
I'll get violent with a pen
From the beginning to the end.
Put the led in their head instead.
And delete the elite with a fleet
Wet them up with sleet mission complete.
These things unheard of and unclear
Where do we go from here.
In these times unsure
If you think you know
That I'm done for
But when you flow
Crime comes more.
We've never been violent
But the friendliest
And still got hate from the envious
Role models are men we missed.
So yes you won't guess
Don't stress
You're so blessed
Pass the whole test

And become the one who knows best
Until the day your soul rests.
For some being real hurts to do
So they throw dirt on you.
They like to pretend though
They only send foes
I'm the type to end those
And let your friends know.
In a new day eat some breakfast
Don't drive reckless
Don't have to like this
But please respect this
Cross that off your checklist.

What I'm Here For

I'm old-school
Steal from me and I'll break your hands
In this life sometimes we have to take a chance
Sorry if I don't do the stuff
That will have them shake and dance
I just write so we can all make a stance
We learn from our mistakes advanced.
So let's start a movement for improvement
Going too fast I might lose them
Men chose God, God didn't choose men.
Think Adam and Eve
Were badder than me
That's what they had them believe
It's sadder to see.
The physical form they don't want to see me in
I may be calm but not lenient
Use a pen or a pencil whatever is convenient.
See I'm about to get rugged
Some of you are going to love it
And start to hug it.
The other half
I look at with my staff
Then start to laugh
Forget numbers I hate math
Now feel my made wrath
On my own I make paths
Away from grimy people
Who need to take baths.
I'm about to roll it
Get my soul lit
And take both hits.
Like I went two for four
You want to do this sure

You'll be the one losing more.
So don't close your palms
Like the UN I'll expose your bombs
Now everyone knows you're calm
When I say you
I don't really mean you
There're some things in life
Everyone's seen too
Just do whatever seems cool
And follow your dreams through
Are you joining my team dude.
Well, here is the storm
They're all misinformed
All the new knowledge isn't born
Yes, they're missing more
That's what I paid this visit for
It's what I'm here for.

What It's For

Now it's not about black or white
It's about people not acting right
So I'm going to bring it back tonight
The reality is we all have to fight.
Most are uninformed
About gun reform
That's what they're coming for
It's why these shootings
Are done some more.
Well the joke's on them
These gun laws they spoke back then.
Since columbine, well they can come for mine
Because I don't own any
Even though I don't hold many
Doesn't mean I don't know plenty.
If you don't like reality
Then learn to dream though
The same weapon was used at San Bernadino.
Even in Aurora you can feel the Aura.
AR used even at a concert in Vegas
Now people laying on dirt outrageous.
Where we at now
Nikolas made it a scary-ass town
My prayers to those families.

When You Aim for Perfection

You know what's funny
Before we make the corrections
We all aim for perfection.
But will never reach it
We'll never achieve it
You better believe it.
Not to bring anyone down
But take a look around
And see what is found.
Before we aim for perfection
Let's aim to be better people
Cut off negativity
And those who are forever evil
Get them out the vicinity.
Let's make the world a better planet
Instead of destroying it
I can't stand it
It's like we planned it
Let's treat one another equally
So we can live legally.
We as minorities
Need to check our priorities
Even if it means
To question Authorities
When you aim for perfection
Aim in all directions
Point at all the sections
So you have no need to make corrections.
Cover all the angles
Because there's nothing
You can't handle.

Make sure everything is right
Before you take flight
If it's a moving target
Move with it but don't discard it
Be prepared before you start it.
They're supposed to be
Your hopes and dreams
But when you're broke it seems
Like you want to give up
Remember it's luck
Sometimes it'll be at your side
To help you thrive and survive
Always keep your pride
And remember to stay alive.
When you aim for perfection.

Words of Wisdom

Everybody wants to go to heaven
But nobody wants to die
It is something
A lot of people have in common why?
If I live life
It wouldn't be on a lie.
Or on something so drastic
I'll end up traumatized
Under the ground in a casket
So I look in my mama's eyes
Before I'm covered in plastic
Watch where the drama lies.
With these words of wisdom
But they were deterred you missed them
When you were referred who listened.
Don't want to be negative
Have a heart to heart with a relative
Tell me if the advice is not well he gives
And figure out an alternative
Always remain alert and attentive
The way we tend to live.
Now I've got to hit you all with my rituals
But touch you with the spirituals
Open your eyes and give you a visual.
Bet they all probably don't care
I keep moving forward
But am getting no where
A piece of me
Is what I won't share
You can have the whole thing
Now you think it's so fair
On second thought
Let's not even go there

As I look at the starry nights
I ask myself are we right
The world will partly fight
The other half hardly might.
I started with my vocals
And my words stay local
But I made them mobile
For them to go global
Too many to add up the total
But I remain noble.
So listen up closely
I'm going to speak on some
But tell you how most be
And it has to be me
Because the gods chose me
The world drugged me
But it couldn't overdose me.
We live in an alpha male sexist society
If you don't like what I tell
I guess you're not taking sides with me.
Teenage boys on barbiturates
The illegal money will switch you quick.
Young girls being promiscuous
All because of TV and magazine influence
The media wants them to get into it
Then criticize your parents on the sins you did.
Things have changed from a year ago
We're going through things
We haven't been through since.
Kids getting shot before class dismissed
How many names pass the list
Of how many at last were missed
What I felt in the past is bliss.

Now I'm going to change the subject
Already said enough
To make them insane and upset.
What I'm saying hate it or love it
I'm going to give you more of it.
Or give you an explanation
Of worldwide degradation
So please pay attention.
No one stays together forever.
High divorce rates
Only so marriage lawyers can get more paid
Off of your court case.
Holy matrimony
Only led to you paying alimony.
Yet she's the one you claimed to adore
Until you walked out the door
Now you're paying child support.
I see to many single parents
But at one point each other is who you cherished.
And that didn't last long enough
Guess it wasn't the strongest love
Why is getting along so tough.
The reality is living in peace is not hard to
But now a difference of opinion
Will make people argue
Built up rage then something starts you.
Feels like something is missing
Only respect for the living.
We have no respect for humanity
The only thing brining us close
Is going through tragedy
We keep submitting to vanity
Real life I don't do parodies.

We want more than what we have
Look at life and start to laugh.
It's all fine and dandy
Until we feel another calamity
Worse than Hurricane Sandy.
Sometimes I look at the sky
Feeling really odd
Asking myself
If there really is such thing as a god
So I put my hand on my face
And start to nod

"Tomorrow makes today yesterday."

About the Author

Edwin Torres was born in Santa Fe, De Bogota, Colombia on July 2, 1983, and migrated to the United States in 1986 with his mother, older sister, and older brother at the age of three. Edwin currently resides in Westchester, New York. He started writing at the age of sixteen. His writings are in a poetry form and reflect on life, love, government, religion, and the world.

9 781646 287239